Bones and Skeletons

Bones and Skeletons

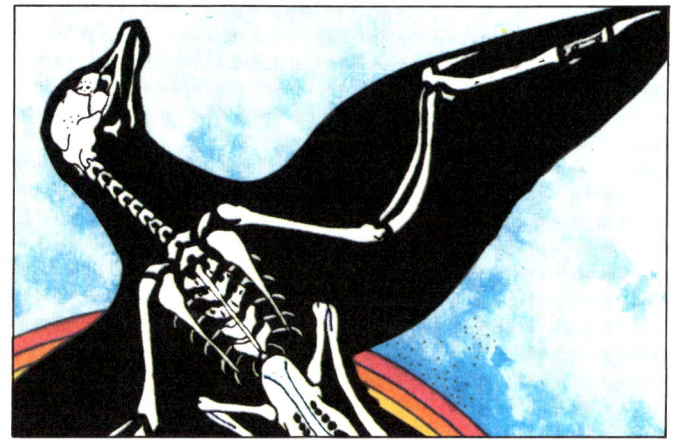

by Brenda Thompson
and
Rosemary Giesen

illustrated by
Carole Viner and Rosemary Giesen

Lerner Publications Company
Minneapolis

Original text by Brenda Thompson
Revised text by Rosemary Giesen
Illustrations by Carole Viner
Additional drawings by Rosemary Giesen

LIBRARY OF CONGRESS CATALOGING IN PUBLICATION DATA

Thompson, Brenda.
  Bones and skeletons.

  (A First Fact Book)
  SUMMARY: Describes the characteristics of human and animal bones and skeletons and the structure of animals without backbones.

  1. Skeleton—Juvenile literature. [1. Skeleton] 1. Giesen, Rosemary, joint author. II. Viner, Carole. III. Title.

QL821.T49 1977   596'.04'7   76-22420
ISBN 0-8225-1352-8

First published 1977 in the United States of America
by Lerner Publications Company

Original edition copyright © 1974 by Sidgwick & Jackson Ltd.
and Brenda Thompson, London. Additional text and illustrations
copyright © 1977 by Lerner Publications Company, Minneapolis.
All rights reserved.

International Standard Book Number: 0-8225-1352-8
Library of Congress Catalog Card Number: 76-22420

2 3 4 5 6 7 8 9 10 85 84 83 82 81 80

You have 206 bones in your body. All of these bones make a frame called a *skeleton.* Pretend that you have no bones. You would be as floppy as a rag doll.

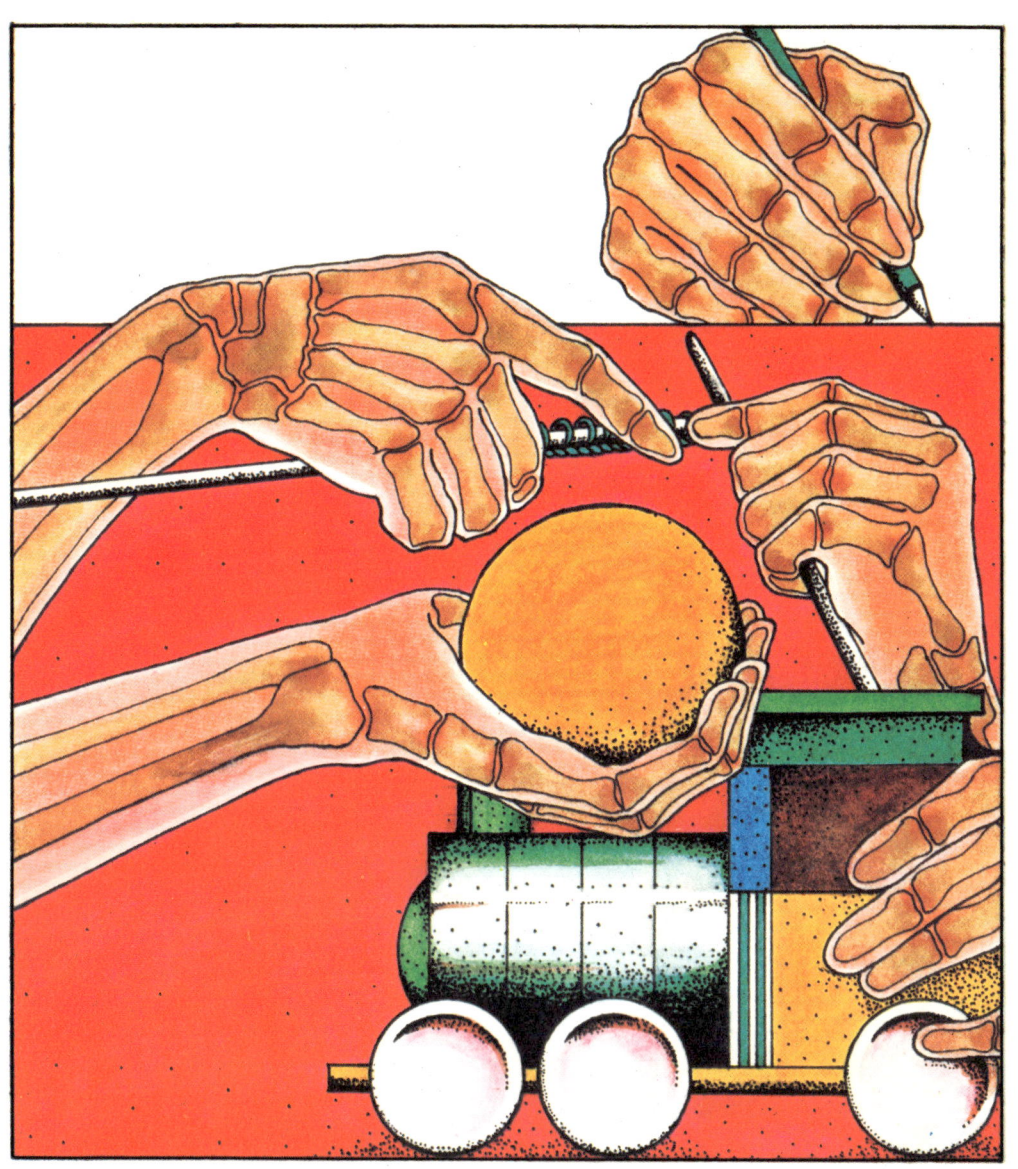

X-ray pictures show all the hidden bones in your body. These bones are held together at places called *joints.* Your hands have many little bones and joints so that you can bend them and pick things up.

Your skull has 22 bones. These bones protect your brain and shape your face. Except for the lower jaw bone, the skull bones are joined in zig-zag joints that do not move.

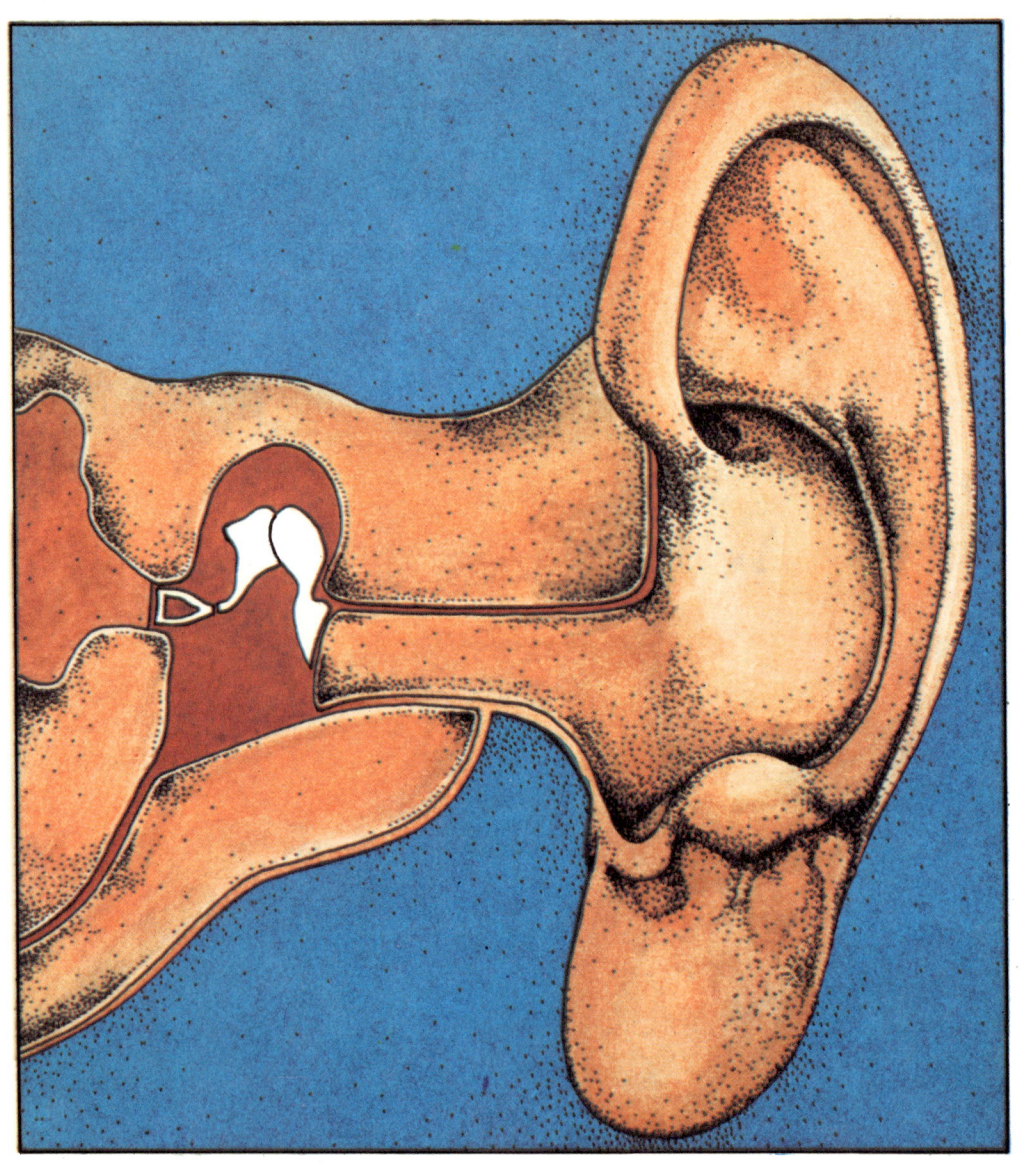

The three bones inside your ear are little but important. They carry sound waves from the eardrum to the inner ear. Without them you could not hear.

The longest and strongest bone in your body is in your thigh. It is called the *femur* (FEE-mer). You need big bones in your legs to carry all your weight.

Many animals also have bones and skeletons. An elephant has a big skeleton to hold up its giant body. See what strong legs it has. They carry a very heavy weight.

The skeleton of a bird is different. A bird's bones are hollow so that the bird is light enough to fly. Air can move through the bird's bones to cool off its body.

A snake has as many as 300 small bones in its backbone! A snake can bend easily because it has many joints.

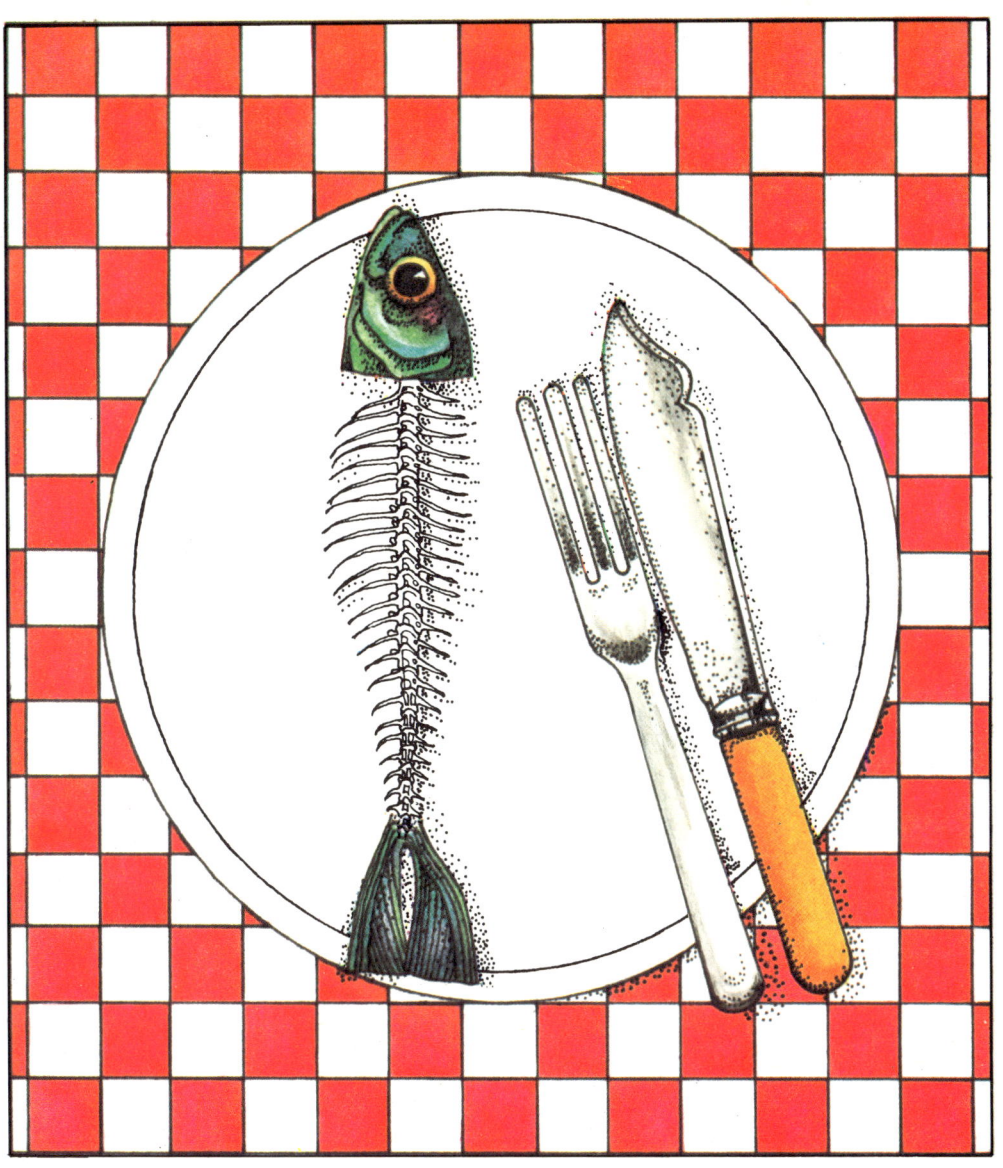

A fish also has many bones and joints along its backbone. When you eat fish, watch out for the little bones!

This animal uses its long tail for support when standing and for balance when hopping. Can you guess what animal it is?

Of course, it is a kangaroo. This strange animal has large, strong hind legs. It can hop at 40 miles (64 kilometers) an hour!

Old bones left behind in the rocks tell us a lot about the large dinosaurs that lived on earth millions of years ago.

Scientists build skeletons from the dinosaur bones they find. Then they can tell what a dinosaur really looked like.

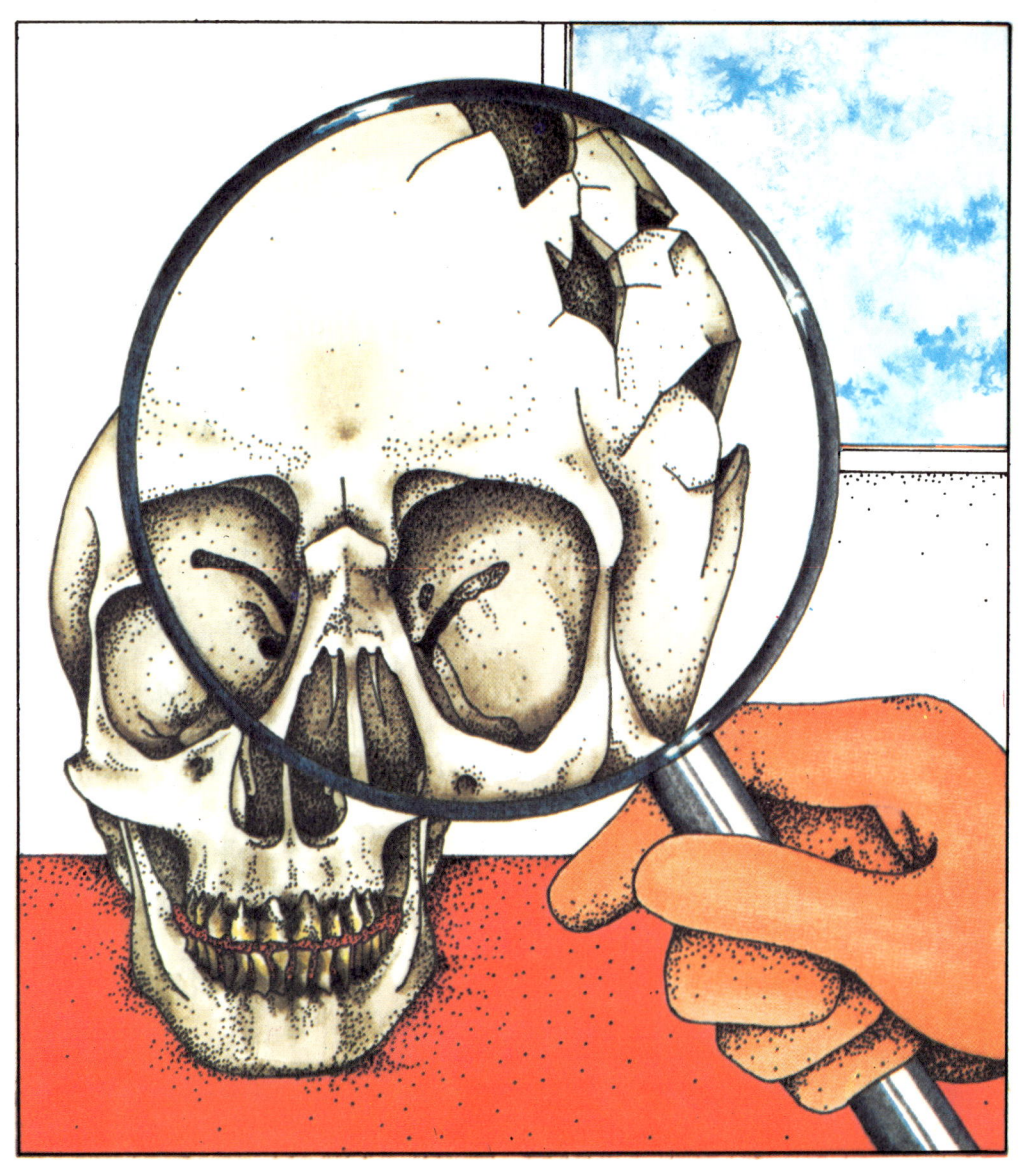

Bones can tell a lot about people and animals of long ago. Can you tell how this man died many years ago?

The holes on his skull show that the man was killed by a battle weapon called a Morning Star.

More About Bones and Skeletons

People and many animals have a backbone as the central part of their skeletons. But not all animals have backbones. Scientists sometimes separate animals into groups of those with backbones and those without. Animals with backbones are called *vertebrates* (VER-tuh-brayts). Those without backbones are called *invertebrates.* There are over 1 million kinds of invertebrates, and about 50,000 kinds of vertebrates.

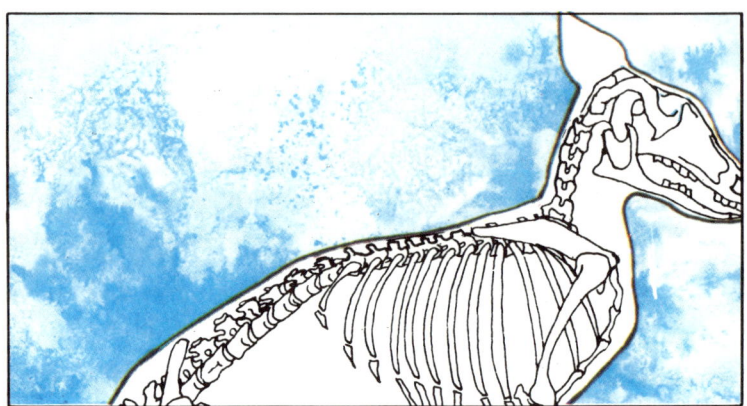

Without a backbone to support their bodies, some invertebrates have no exact shape. The tiny amoeba (uh-MEE-buh) is a shapeless mass of living matter in a thin, clear skin. Because an amoeba has no bones or skeleton, it is always changing shape as it moves.

Amoeba

A sponge is like an amoeba because it, too, has no exact shape. But a sponge does have a skeleton. Its skeleton is not made of bones, but of many tiny needles or fibers.

Sponge

Other invertebrates also have skeletons, but no bones. The shells of clams, snails, and oysters are really the skeletons of these animals. They are said to have *exoskeletons.* Exoskeletons are skeletons on the outside of animals' bodies.

Snail

The shells of clams, snails, and oysters protect their soft bodies. When an enemy is near, these soft animals can go into their shells to safety.

Clam

Like clams and oysters, insects also have exoskeletons. Their hard suits of armor are lighter and stronger than bone. Insects' skeletons protect their bodies. An insect's skeleton is made of many parts that meet at joints. This lets the insect bend and move around.

Ant

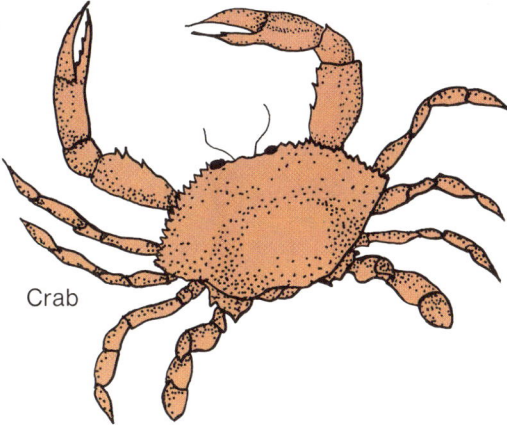

Crabs and lobsters also have a hard-shelled skeleton on the outside of their bodies. Like insect skeletons, their skeletons are in parts. At the joints the shell is softer so that a crab or a lobster can bend.

Crab

List of New Words

amoeba	oyster
exoskeleton	skeleton
femur	skull
invertebrate	sponge
joint	vertebrate

A Message to Educators

Children who have just learned to read have entered a world filled with new pleasure and knowledge. They have begun a journey that will take them to distant times, to far-away lands, and to the mysterious territory inside their own minds. The *First Fact Books* are designed to help young readers get a good start on that life-long journey. Originally conceived by Brenda Thompson, a British educator and author, the series provides a first look at a variety of topics drawn from the fields of science and history. Each book makes use of vivid, full-color illustrations that serve to attract and hold the young reader's interest. The simply written text satisfies that interest by presenting basic facts about the subject in a manner that is both stimulating and informative. In addition, each book includes a section containing supplementary information for those readers who want to expand their knowledge. Designed for both classroom use and independent study, the *First Fact Books* provide children with an early learning experience that is both enjoyable and rewarding.